EVENTS THAT CHANGED YOUR WORLD

ALEXANDER GRAHAM BELL INVENTS THE TELEPHONE

by Rachel Werner

a Capstone company — publishers for children

Raintree is an imprint of Capstone Global Library Limited, a company incorporated in England and Wales having its registered office at 264 Banbury Road, Oxford, OX2 7DY – Registered company number: 6695582

www.raintree.co.uk
myorders@raintree.co.uk

Copyright © 2025 Capstone Global Library Limited
The moral rights of the proprietor have been asserted.

All rights reserved. No part of this publication may be reproduced in any form or by any means (including photocopying or storing it in any medium by electronic means and whether or not transiently or incidentally to some other use of this publication) without the written permission of the copyright owner, except in accordance with the provisions of the Copyright, Designs and Patents Act 1988 or under the terms of a licence issued by the Copyright Licensing Agency, 5th Floor, Shackleton House, 4 Battle Bridge Lane, London SE1 2HX (www.cla.co.uk). Applications for the copyright owner's written permission should be addressed to the publisher.

Editorial credits
Edited by Ericka Smith
Designed by Terri Poburka
Production by Katy LaVigne

Acknowledgements
We would like to thank the following for permission to reproduce photographs: Alamy: GL Archive, 16, North Wind Picture Archives, 6; Getty Images: Archive Photos/Pictorial Parade, 22, Bettmann, 13, Dorling Kindersley, 28, Fox Photos, cover (bottom), 19, Kerkez, 27, Nick Dolding, 24; Library of Congress: 5, 12; Newscom: abacausa/Graylock, 25, Oronoz/Album, 17; Shutterstock: akilasaki, 11, Alena Ozerova, cover (top), Corner Photography, 23, Everett Collection, 9, 10, 20; SuperStock: Classic Picture Library/SC, 21, Science and Society/SSPL/Science Museum, 14, Universal Images/Picturenow, 15

Direct quotation: Page 18, from April 1999, *Library of Congress* article "'Mr Watson, Come Here'", loc.gov

978 1 3982 5985 0

British Library Cataloguing in Publication Data
A full catalogue record for this book is available from the British Library.

All product and company names are trademarks™ or registered® trademarks of their respective holders.

All the internet addresses (URLs) given in this book were valid at the time of going to press. However, due to the dynamic nature of the internet, some addresses may have changed, or sites may have changed or ceased to exist since publication. While the author and publisher regret any inconvenience this may cause readers, no responsibility for any such changes can be accepted by either the author or the publisher.

Printed and bound in India.

CONTENTS

Teacher turned inventor **4**
Signals and letters **6**
The first telephone call **12**
Phoning into the future **22**

Timeline 29
Glossary 30
Find out more 31
Index 32
About the author 32

Words in **bold** are in the glossary.

Teacher turned inventor

Today, a world without phones is hard to imagine. But the telephone was only invented about 150 years ago. Alexander Graham Bell's experiments on **transmitting** sound led to its invention. He **patented** the telephone in 1876.

Bell's telephone changed how people communicated. And its usefulness quickly grew beyond anything he could have imagined.

Signals and letters

People have always been able to communicate over long distances. Smoke and fire signals were a part of many cultures. In 150 BCE, the ancient Greeks began using smoke signals to represent their alphabet. This made smoke signals easier to understand.

Ancient Greeks sending signals with smoke

People also communicated by using light patterns or flag positions to represent letters and numbers. This system is called **semaphore**. It was often used during times of war, such as during the French Revolution (1789–1799).

Did you know?

Chinese soldiers in China during the Ming dynasty (1368–1644) would keep watch on the Great Wall of China. They sent messages along the wall to each other using smoke signals.

By the 1700s, more people could read and write. Letter writing became the main way to communicate. But sending letters in the post could take weeks or even months. A letter had to travel by horse, stagecoach, boat or train before reaching its destination.

The **Industrial Revolution** changed many people's everyday lives. The use of machines increased. Suddenly, **inventors** had new parts, such as lights and wiring, to tinker with. Benjamin Franklin demonstrated that electricity could be channelled into an object to move or operate it.

Franklin experimenting with electricity

Franklin's discovery helped bring about the **telegraph**. Samuel Morse created this machine in the 1830s. A telegraph could transmit messages over a wire from one city to another. These messages were called telegrams.

Samuel Morse with his telegraph

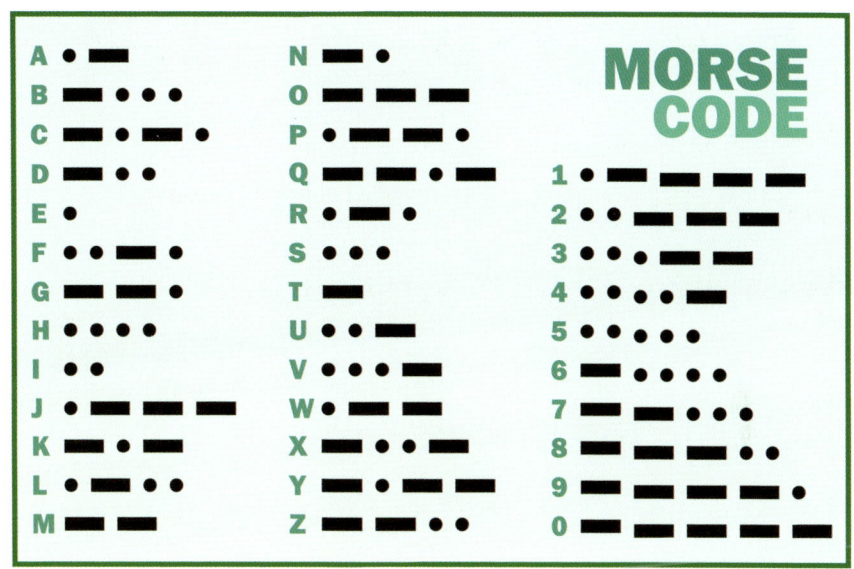

Different electrical pulses sent by a telegraph corresponded to different numbers and letters. This system was called Morse code.

For many years, sending a telegram was the fastest way to communicate. Then, Alexander Graham Bell invented the telephone.

The first telephone call

Scottish-born inventor Bell was born and educated in Edinburgh. Later, his family moved to Canada. In 1871, Bell moved to the United States to work at the Boston School for Deaf **Mutes**. He went there to teach "visible speech".

Visible speech used symbols to represent sounds. It helped people say words in any language. Bell taught deaf people how to move their mouths to make sounds.

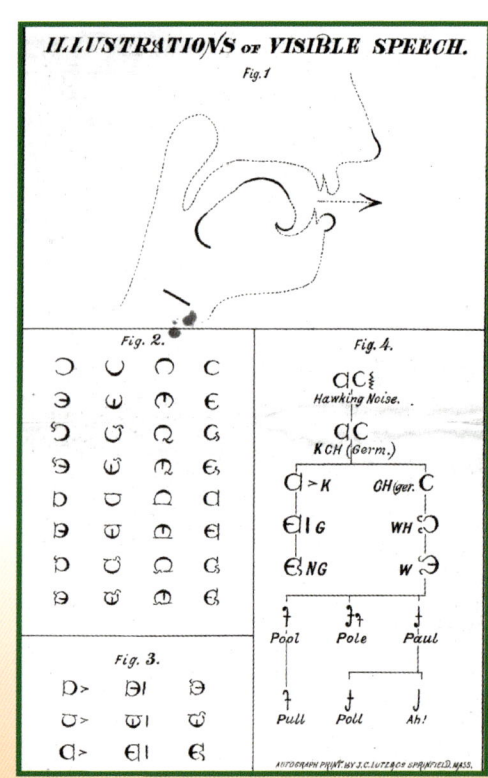

Bell teaching a deaf girl to speak

While in Boston, Bell also worked on methods for sending more than one telegraph message at the same time on one line. This work produced a machine called a harmonic telegraph. It used reeds or tuning forks that picked up certain sounds. It could transmit several sounds at the same time.

Bell's harmonic telegraph

14

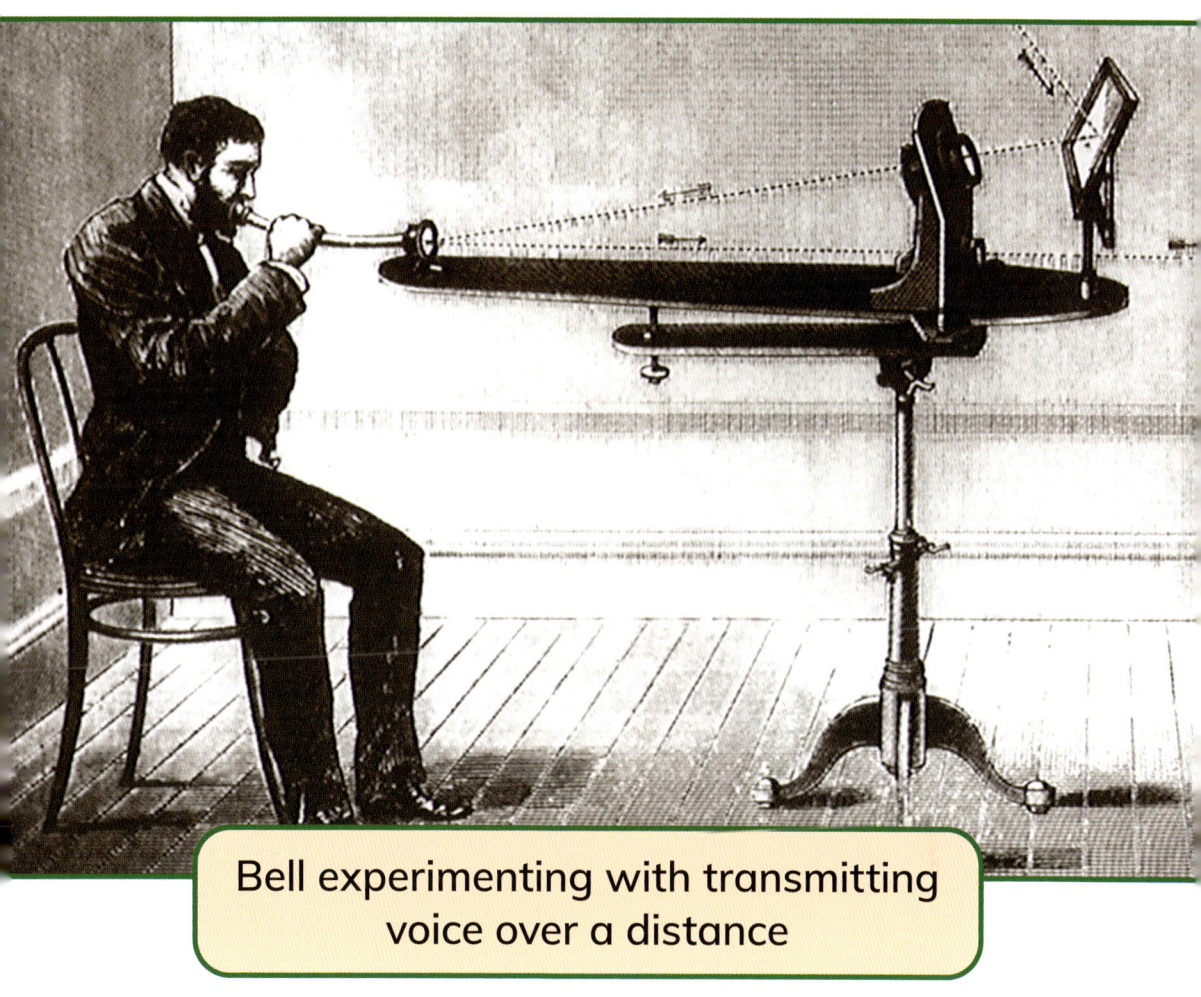

Bell experimenting with transmitting voice over a distance

This got Bell interested in creating a device that could transmit a person's voice – a "speaking telegraph". He started experimenting.

Bell found two men to help him. One was Lewis Latimer. He was a self-taught **draftsman**. Bell hired Latimer to create drawings of his telephone design. The other helper was Thomas Watson. Watson helped Bell work out the mechanical problems with his design.

Lewis Latimer

Bell (left) and Watson

Latimer and Watson helped Bell create a transmitter for his next **prototype** that produced better sound quality. Voices came through clear enough to be understood.

On 14 February 1876, Bell's lawyers put in an application for a patent for Bell's telephone. Just a few weeks later, Bell made his first call. It was on 10 March that Bell called Watson, who was in a nearby room. "Mr. Watson – come here – I want to see you," he said to Watson.

In 1915, Watson would also be on the other end of the line when Bell placed the first call from one end of a continent to another. The call was made from New York to San Francisco in the United States.

Bell making a call from New York City to Chicago in 1892

Did you know?

Bell was not the only inventor trying to create an early prototype of the telephone. Elisha Gray, Bell's rival, applied for a patent for a similar machine on the same day as Bell's lawyers.

Bell had made it possible for people on opposite sides of the continent to speak. But what about calling a friend across the Atlantic Ocean? This was the next project for Bell's team of researchers, now working at Bell Laboratories.

A man using a telephone around 1920

The first transatlantic telephone call

By the late 1920s, Bell's team felt confident that radio waves could be used instead of electrical wires to transmit sound to a telephone. The first official transatlantic call happened on 7 January 1927. It was between New York City and London.

Phoning into the future

More people had access to telephones throughout the 20th century. Public pay phones became common, especially in cities.

A public phone in Japan in 1955

Party lines – telephone lines that connected every home in a local area – provided an affordable phone service. They were useful in **rural** areas. But neighbours could listen in on each other's calls.

The types of phones people use have changed over time. Rotary, push-button and cordless phones were all popular home phones.

A rotary phone

In the 1970s, the telephone would get its biggest makeover yet. The mobile phone was created. The first mobile phone call was made in 1973. However, mobile phones weren't available to the public until 1984.

A mobile phone from the 1980s

One of the scientists working at Bell's company during this time was Dr Shirley Ann Jackson. Her research helped develop several technologies, including touch-tone phones, caller ID, call waiting and **fibre-optic** cables. Fibre-optic cables help to provide fast internet service.

Dr Shirley Ann Jackson

Another person who worked for Bell's company is Jesse Russell. His ideas helped to create the smartphone.

Smartphones also changed how a phone could be used – and by whom. Touchscreens made phones more user-friendly. This was especially good for disabled people, children and the elderly. Today, many phone apps help us connect and chat with people all around the world.

Thanks to Bell, phones have changed much of our day-to-day lives. They affect how we learn, play, work, travel and shop. And most importantly, they help us connect with each other.

Timeline

1844	Samuel Morse sends a telegram using the first public telegraph system.
1871	Alexander Graham Bell starts working at the Boston School for Deaf Mutes.
1876	Bell builds his first working telephone.
1877	Bell starts the Bell Telephone Company.
1884	The first pay phone is installed.
1885	Bell Telephone Company becomes the American Telephone and Telegraph Company (AT&T).
1927	The first transatlantic phone call is made between New York City and London.
1956	The cordless phone is invented.
1973	The first public call is made by mobile phone.
1992	IBM invents the first smartphone.
1997	Mobile game and social media apps are first released.

Glossary

draftsman someone who draws plans for something, such as machinery or a building

fibre-optic made of thin fibres of glass in bundles that send information as light

Industrial Revolution period starting in the mid-1700s when work started to be done by machines

inventor person who thinks of new ideas, devices or methods

mute unable or unwilling to speak

patent legal document giving the inventor of an item the sole rights to make or sell it

prototype first version of an invention that tests an idea to see if it will work

rural far from towns or cities

semaphore system of sending messages using flags or lights

telegraph machine that uses electrical signals to send messages over long distances

transmit send

Find out more

Books

Inventions: A Children's Encyclopedia, DK (DK, 2018)

Inventors: Incredible Stories of the World's Most Ingenious Inventions, Robert Winston (DK Children, 2020)

The Book of Inventions: Discover Brilliant Ideas from Fascinating People, Tim Cooke (Welbeck Publishing, 2020)

Websites

www.bbc.co.uk/bitesize/articles/z6kg3j6#zwdqjsg
Learn more about the Industrial Revolution with BBC Bitesize.

www.bbc.co.uk/teach/class-clips-video/articles/zf7gd6f
Watch this BBC Teach video about Alexander Graham Bell.

www.twinkl.co.uk/teaching-wiki/history-of-the-telephone
Discover more about the history of the telephone.

Index

Boston, USA 14
Boston School for Deaf Mutes 12
Canada 12
Chicago, USA 19
Edinburgh 12
Franklin, Benjamin 8–10
French Revolution 7
Gray, Elisha 19
Great Wall of China 7
Greeks 6
harmonic telegraph 14
Industrial Revolution 8
Jackson, Shirley Ann 25
Latimer, Lewis 16–17
London 21
Ming dynasty 7
Morse code 11
Morse, Samuel 10
New York City, USA 18, 19, 21
Russell, Jesse 26
San Francisco, USA 18
Scotland 12
semaphore 7
smoke signals 6, 7
visible speech 12–13
Watson, Thomas 16–17, 18

About the author

Rachel Werner is the author of many books, including *Floods*, *Moving and Grooving to Filmore's Beat*, *The Glam World Tour* and *Glow & Grow: A Brown Girl's Positive Body Guide*. She lives in the United States. She is associated with Hugo House in Seattle, Lighthouse Writers Workshop in Denver and the Loft Literary Center in Minneapolis, where she leads curricula to educate writers and content producers in marketing their work.